To . . . .

From . . . .

OTHER BOOKS IN THE TO-GIVE-AND-TO-KEEP® SERIES:

To a very Special Dad	To a very Special Sister
To a very Special Daughter	To a very Special Son
To a very Special Friend	Welcome to the New Baby
To a very Special Grandpa	Wishing you Happiness
Happy Anniversary	To a special couple on your Wedding Day
To my very Special Husband	To a very special Grandson
To my very Special Love	To a very special Teacher
To a very Special Mother	To a very Special Grandmother

Published simultaneously in 1993 by Helen Exley Giftbooks LLC in the USA and Helen Exley Giftbooks in Great Britain.

12 11 10 9 8 7 6

Illustrations copyright © Helen Exley 1993, 2002
Selection copyright © Helen Exley 1993, 2002
The moral right of the author has been asserted.

ISBN 1-86187-368-9

Edited by Helen Exley.
Printed in China.

Acknowledgements: Roger McGough, "Happiness", copyright 1973 by the author, from Gig, published by Cape 1973. Reprinted by permission of the author and publishers; Edwin Muir, "The Confirmation", from Collected Poems, Faber and Faber Ltd. Reprinted by permission of the publishers.

Helen Exley Giftbooks, 16 Chalk Hill, Watford, Herts WD19 4BG, United Kingdom
Helen Exley Giftbooks LLC, 185 Main Street, Spencer, MA 01562, USA.
www.helenexleygiftbooks.com

To *my very special*
WIFE

A Helen Exley Giftbook
Illustrations by Juliette Clarke

No cord or cable can draw so forcibly,
or bind so fast, as love can do with
a single thread.

ROBERT BURTON (1577-1640)

▥EXLEY

ONLY YOU

Tis you alone that sweetens life, and makes one

wish the wings of time were clipt, which not only

seems but really flies away too fast, much too fast,

for those that love....

JOHN HERVEY
to his wife, Elizabeth

. . .

She gave me eyes, she gave me ears;

And humble cares, and delicate fears;

A heart, the fountain of sweet tears;

And love, and thought, and joy.

WILLIAM WORDSWORTH (1770-1850)

. . .

[She is] ... one that to her husband is more than a friend, less than trouble; an equal with him in the yoke. Calamities and troubles she shares alike, nothing pleases her that doth not him. She is relative in all, and he without her is but half himself. She is his absent hands, eyes, ears and mouth; his present and absent all ... a husband without her is a misery to man's apparel....

SIR THOMAS OVERBURY (1581-1613)

. . .

There are actually many females in the world, and some among them are beautiful. But where could I find again a face, whose every feature, even every wrinkle, is a reminder of the greatest and sweetest memories of my life? Even my endless pains, my irreplaceable losses I read in your sweet face.

KARL MARX (1818-1883)
in a letter to his wife, Jenny

. . .

WITH MY LOVE

I learned the real meaning of love. Love is absolute loyalty. People fade, looks fade, but loyalty never fades. You can depend so much on certain people, you can set your watch by them. And that's love, even if it doesn't seem very exciting.

SYLVESTER STALLONE

. . .

The supreme happiness of life is the conviction of being loved for yourself, or, more correctly, being loved in spite of yourself.

VICTOR HUGO (1802-1885)

. . .

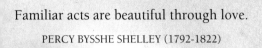

Familiar acts are beautiful through love.

PERCY BYSSHE SHELLEY (1792-1822)

. . .

Left alone, Levin asked himself again if he really felt any regret for the freedom his friends had been talking about.

The idea made him smile.

"Freedom? What do I need freedom for? Happiness for me consists in loving, in thinking Kitty's thoughts and wishing her wishes, without any freedom."

LEO TOLSTOY
from *"Anna Karenina"*

. . .

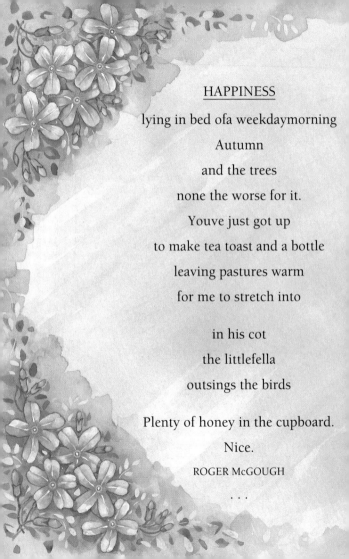

HAPPINESS

lying in bed ofa weekdaymorning

Autumn

and the trees

none the worse for it.

Youve just got up

to make tea toast and a bottle

leaving pastures warm

for me to stretch into

in his cot

the littlefella

outsings the birds

Plenty of honey in the cupboard.

Nice.

ROGER McGOUGH

. . .

MY HEART'S FRIEND

Fair is the white star of twilight,
  And the sky cleaner
    At the day's end;
But she is fairer, and she is dearer,
  She, my heart's friend!

Fair is the white star of twilight,
  And the moon roving
    To the sky's end;
But she is fairer, better worth loving,
  She, my heart's friend.

Shoshone Love Song

. . .

COME LIVE WITH ME

Come live with me, and be my love,

And we will some new pleasures prove

Of golden sands, and crystal brooks,

With silken lines, and silver hooks.

JOHN DONNE (1573-1631)

. . .

I will give my love an apple without e'er a core,

I will give my love a house without e'er a door,

I will give my love a palace wherein she may be,

And she may unlock it without any key.

My head is the apple without e'er a core,

My mind is the house without e'er a door,

My heart is the palace wherein she may be,

And she may unlock it without any key.

Folk Song

. . .

As you are woman, so be lovely,

As you are lovely, so be various,

Merciful as constant, constant as various,

So be mine, as I yours for ever.

ROBERT GRAVES (1895-1985)

. . .

A GOOD MARRIAGE

How much the wife is dearer than the bride.

GEORGE LYTTLETON (1719-1773)

. . .

What is there in the vale of life

Half so delightful as a wife,

When friendship, love, and peace combine

To stamp the marriage bond divine?

WILLIAM COWPER

. . .

I think a man and a woman should choose
each other for life, for the simple reason
that a long life with all its accidents is barely
enough for a man and a woman to understand
each other; and in this case to understand
is to love.

JOHN BUTLER YEATS

. . .

When one has once fully entered the realm of love,
the world - no matter how imperfect - becomes rich
and beautiful, for it consists solely of
opportunities for love.

SOREN KIERKEGAARD (1813-1855)

. . .

There is no applause in marriage.
No one applauds a flowering tree.

HAROLD PHILIPS

. . .

ALL FOR YOU

She is mine to have and to hold!

She has chosen between love and gold!

All the joys life can give

Shall be hers, while I live,

For she's mine to have and to hold.

WILL A. HEELAN

. . .

To believe in a woman, to make her your

religion, the fount of life, the secret

luminary of all your least thoughts - is this

not second birth?

HONORÉ DE BALZAC

. . .

...As for me, to love you alone, to make you happy, to do nothing which would contradict your wishes, this is my destiny and the aim of my life. Be happy, do not concern yourself about me; do not interest yourself in the happiness of a man who lives only in your life, who enjoys only your pleasures, your happiness. When I require from you love such as mine, I do wrong.... When I sacrifice to you all my desires, all my thoughts, all the moments of my life, I yield to the ascendancy which your charms, your character, your whole being has gained over my wretched heart.

NAPOLEON BONAPARTE
from a letter to Josephine

WHAT IS A WIFE?

She's the only one who knows exactly how and
where to scratch your back.

GERALD PARKINSON

. . .

They must be something. Why else would all these
millions of hulking great men go down on their
knees to get only one each?

G. MARKS

. . .

They're magic. Who else can mend the television
with a kick?

J. BATES

. . .

A wife is a spiky, complex creature brought
into conjunction with another spiky,
complex creature. For the rest of their
lives they will be working out how to fit
into the small world of marriage without
damaging each other.

JIMMY MEACHER

. . .

To find out what a wife is, go back to Mother
for a couple of days.
You'll soon realize what the missing ingredient is.

M. STRATFORD

. . .

A PEACE, A CALM

There is no happy life

But in a wife;

The comforts are so sweet

When they do meet:

'Tis plenty, peace, a calm

Like dropping balm:...

WILLIAM CAVENDISH (1592-1676)

. . .

When a man of thirty-five is happily, blissfully married, the scope of his reflections is necessarily limited.... He is no longer haunted by the face of every pretty girl he meets, for he has already met the woman most fitted in the wide world to make him happy.... He is no longer prone to dreams about the object of his affections, for he has her perpetually beside him.

ROBERT GRANT
from *"Reflections of a Married Man"*, 1892

. . .

UNCHANGING LOVE

If twenty years were to be erased and I were to be presented with the same choice again under the same circumstances I would act precisely as I did then.... Perhaps I needed her even more in those searing lonely moments when I - I alone knew in my heart what my decision must be. I have needed her all these 20 years. I love her and need her now.

I always will.

DUKE OF WINDSOR
about his wife

. . .

I'll love you dear, I'll love you

Till China and Africa meet,

And the river jumps over the mountain

And the salmon sing in the street.

I'll love you till the ocean

Is folded and hung up to dry

And the seven stars go squawking

Like geese about the sky.

W. H. AUDEN

. . .

You ought to trust me for I do not love and will

never love any woman in the world but you, and my

chief desire is to link myself to you week by week by

bonds which shall ever become more intimate and

profound.

Beloved I kiss your memory - your sweetness and

beauty have cast a glory upon my life.

SIR WINSTON CHURCHILL (1874-1965)
from a letter to his wife, Clementine

. . .

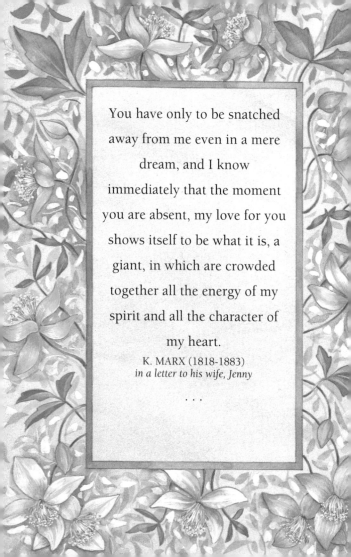

You have only to be snatched
away from me even in a mere
dream, and I know
immediately that the moment
you are absent, my love for you
shows itself to be what it is, a
giant, in which are crowded
together all the energy of my
spirit and all the character of
my heart.

K. MARX (1818-1883)
in a letter to his wife, Jenny

. . .

WITHOUT HER

Without her laughter a room full of babbling people
feels cold and empty.

N. NAIDOO

. . .

They all think I'm tough, successful, even macho.
Only she knows. I'm weak, I'm like a lost puppy
without her.

HUGH COTTRELL

. . .

I can pack just as well as she can. But she doesn't
forget my tooth-brush.

PETER SIMONS

. . .

Without Judy I'd suddenly feel forty-one years, two
months and eleven days old, after all.

ROBERT NORTH

. . .

MY WIFE

Trusty, dusky, vivid true,

With eyes of gold and bramble-dew,

Steel true and blade-straight,

The great artificer

Made my mate.

Honour, anger, valour, fire,

A love that life could never tire,

Death quench or evil stir;

The mighty master

Gave to her.

Teacher, tender, comrade, wife,

A fellow-farer true through life,

Heart-whole and soul-free,

the august father

Gave to me.

ROBERT LOUIS STEVENSON (1850-1894)

. . .

THE CONFIRMATION

Yes, yours, my love, is the right human face.

I in my mind had waited for this long,

Seeing the false and searching for the true,

Then found you as a traveller finds a place

Of welcome suddenly amid the wrong

Valleys and rocks and twisting roads. But you,

What shall I call you? A fountain in a waste,

A well of water in a country dry,

Or anything that's honest and good, an eye

That makes the whole world bright. Your open heart,

Simple with giving, gives the primal deed,

The first good world, the blossom, the blowing seed,

The hearth, the steadfast land, the wandering sea,

Not beautiful or rare in every part,

But like yourself, as they were meant to be.

EDWIN MUIR (1887-1959)

. . .

TOGETHER ALWAYS

When she consented to dance, the first time I
met her, I held her hand.

In cinemas, on country walks, I held her hand.

When promising to love and cherish, I
held her hand.

When each child was born, I held her hand.
Such small hands! Golden hands! Amazingly
creative - to economize. Hard worked and
roughened they may have been, but only
smoothness was sensed in her caressing.

Now the hands are blue-veined, drawn
white but still active. Cool on my fevered
head, warm and comforting when
I am down. And if we go to the church or
shop, in fact anywhere I always hold that
precious hand.

GEORGE SOMERVILLE

. . .

I'd choose her again anytime,
anywhere. Put her in a crowd of
beautiful, intelligent girls and I'd
choose her. That's because she's
good for me and her tum doesn't put
my middle-age spread to shame.

DAVE MASON

. . .

She runs her fingers through my hair
like she did when we were courting
even though I've only three left.

A. BOURNE

. . .

Grow old along with me!
The best is yet to be,
The last of life, for which the
first was made.

MATTHEW ARNOLD (1822-1888)

. . .